A Journey of the Heart

To Dianna

Bonnie

A Journey of the Heart

Life's Trials and Triumphs Seen Through Poetry

Bonnie Hopson

ABUNDANT HARVEST
PUBLISHING

Editing/Formatting: Erik V. Sahakian
Cover Design/Layout: Andrew Enos

All Scripture is taken from the New King James Version of the
Bible. Copyright © 1979, 1980, 1982 by Thomas Nelson, Inc.
Used by permission. All rights reserved.

Library of Congress Control Number: 2021919071

ISBN 978-1-7377261-0-4
First Printing: October 2021

FOR INFORMATION CONTACT:

Abundant Harvest Publishing
35145 Oak Glen Rd
Yucaipa, CA 92399
www.abundantharvestpublishing.com

Printed in the United States of America

This book is dedicated to my Mother and Father and Sister who are with Jesus now. Thank you to each one for loving me. Until we meet again, you will always be in my heart.

Contents

Preface

This is a journey of my heart and the things in my life I have experienced. Writing how I feel has brought a healing of my heart as I walk this path that God has given me. Of course, there have also been many happy times. I am grateful, thankful, and blessed for every season.

I hope this book will help you on your journey in life. Remember, you'll never walk alone for our Lord walks with you all the days of your life.

Bonnie Hopson

A Girl's First Horse

Young and spirited like me,
Comanche was a mustang,
wild and free.

When I called his name he came to me;
he nuzzled me with his muzzle
as if to say, "Let's go!"

And so I climbed up on his back
and off we rode through the desert
with the wind at our back.

His gallop was smooth and easy
as though he had wings to carry us.
Just a girl and her horse—
two spirits running free.

Oh, My Soul

Some say I have no soul; they really don't know.
For if they would look into my eyes they would
see how much love I have to give.

I see for those who cannot.
I hear for those that can't hear.
I lay and comfort those who have endured wars.
I seek and alert before a seizure.
I protect and serve you, putting my life at risk.
And with all this, I love you unconditionally.

So many could learn from a dog.
After all, God named every living thing.
God spelled backward.

So look into my eyes and tell me I have no soul.

Thanksgiving Prayer for the Pets

Father, all creatures belong to You;
they are in Your loving care.
They give their unconditional love
as You have given us Yours.

I ask You to keep them safe from all harm.
I pray for Your eternal love in the companionship
and friendship that this pet provides.

Please help the ones that are alone
to find their forever home with a loving family.
Amen!

No Greater Love

We huddle at night and wait for dawn's early light.
To walk again not knowing where,
but in God's trust I keep you near.

They say I have a place to live.
I say, "Thank you; may he stay too?"
"No," he replies, "only for you."
So I turn and walk away.

I look down at you as you give me your paw.
Oh, my faithful friend of so many years.
I will find the courage behind my tears.

So our journey continues, my four-pawed-friend,
as I promised you, from beginning to end.

I Am Free

Please don't cry for me, for now I'm free.
I have followed the path God set for me.
As you lay upon your pillow at night
with tears that fill your eyes.
Remember how I slept with you
and cuddled through the night.

Your gentle touch, my life was full,
you gave so much.
But you see God needed me more.
So I will patiently await,
until you pass through Heaven's gate.

The Vigil

A dog lay dead, hit by a car,
speeding along down the street.
A little spaniel ran to his side,
and sat right down at his feet.

Keeping vigil all through the night,
and well past the break of day.
Guarding a pal, he would not leave,
until kind friends led him away.

A look of grief came to his eyes;
grief for a life that had fled.
For instinct seemed to let him know,
that his little pal was dead.

Surely he had a heart of gold,
ever faithful until the end.
Keeping guard through the night and cold,
watching, protecting a friend.

This is a lesson taught by a dog,
one that we shall heed.

Faith, devotion, brotherly love;
yes! This is a lesson indeed.

My Sister

My sister is so strong and courageous;
she amazes me every day.
Her challenges have been many,
but defeats each one without dismay.

My sister holds fast to her faith
that this must be just a part of life,
but she never shows strife.

So many times we wish for a different life;
yet, my sister never complains
of what's been dealt her.

If I could take her place,
I would do just that.
To ease her pain because, hey,
she's my sister.

Wings of Valor

What man is this that without hesitation
climbs in his plane, knowing there is no fame
in doing what he is asked to do?

To protect and serve our country
is what's in his head.
He flies on faith for God has given him
wings to fight the battles to come,
knowing he will win.

So who is this man of valor
of 100 missions and more?
This was my father
that I will love forevermore.

Heart of Gold

There you stood, one blue eye, one brown,
and a heart upon your shoulder you wore so proud.
A heart of gold, you gave your all through
snow storm we rode, you protected me well.

The rodeo came, we made the drill team,
day and night you gave it your all.
You were always ready to meet the crowd.
You never failed me, my Heart of Gold.

The quiet times, just you and I,
through meadows we would go
and sit upon a hill,
and watch the deer roam.

Cattle came and cattle went;
oh, how you roped them well.
Now run in Heaven, run well,
until we meet again, my Heart of Gold.

Majestic Skies

I say to you, never look down but always up.
For the clouds have many colors,
so majestic are they.

God has painted them for you and I to enjoy.
He is the artist of the earth and sky,
and of our lives.

So look up to those majestic skies,
for He is our master,
the creator of our lives.

You Will Never Walk Alone

You will never walk alone
for God is on the throne.
The day God took you home,
I never felt so alone.

He knows our chapters, one by one,
for He is the author of our lives.
Every chapter full of memories—
times of joy and tears, triumphs and defeats.

Through every passing year,
my Mommy, an angel with love
I cannot say in words;
there'll never be another.

Help me, Lord, to keep alive her memory
and never let me walk alone.

I Am Not Gone, Just Away

Thank you, master,
for taking care of me.
But now it is time
to set me free.

In the still of the night,
I will gently lay.
And promise
to never stray.

And as morning breaks,
go about your day.
For I am not gone,
I am just away.

Though you cannot see me,
this is true.
But my paw print
lives in you.

Please take the walks
we used to do.

And know that I
will wait for you.

For I am not gone,
I am just away.
Only to see you
another day.

Moonlight

I stood beside a rippling stream,
and gazed at harvest moon.
The night was still, the air was cool,
and the world was all in tune.

A mantle of light encircled me,
and kissed the autumn trees.
Each little leaf seemed to shine,
as it bowed in the evening breeze.

Twinkling stars like lanterns aglow,
glistened high above.
And in the stillness of the night,
came tender thoughts of love.

I felt the spell of a magic touch,
and heard a soft, sweet voice.
It said love rules the universe,
for God is love—rejoice!

My heart then beat with sudden joy,
there on the soft green grass.

In the silvery moonlight, then I knew,
the founder of love is God.

Only a Dog

Only a dog, oh what a friend,
with nature so noble and true.
When your friends are scattered and gone,
he is the one that will stick by you.

Just a kind word is all that he asks,
and the pat of his master's hand,
will fill his heart with love and joy.
He knows and can understand.

You may be rich, or you may be poor;
he is with you in either case.
For rags or riches mean nothing to him;
it's the smile on his master's face.

If the cupboard is empty and bare,
no bones to put on his plate,
he just comes over to lick your hand,
and seemingly says, "I can wait."

When night comes on and you go to rest,
he crawls up on his bed.

You can sleep tight all through the night,
for he'll keep watch that everything's alright.

Only a dog, but what if he is?
He will stick till the end of time.
What more can anyone ask of him?
A dog is a best friend indeed.

Only a dog, but he understands,
so well that his nature will blend.
When you are blue,
then he is too.

Only a dog, so be kind to him,
for he has a lovable creed.
Trust and devotion, greater than man's,
a dog is a friend indeed.

Through the Storm

When you walk through the storm,
hold your head up high.
And lift your hands
to our God in the sky.

For God wants us to have faith
to overcome our fears.
For He is always near.

At the end of the storm
there is a golden sky,
and He will heal the land.
For God wants us to have faith
to overcome our fears.

So walk on with hope in your heart
and you will never walk alone.
For God promises that.

An Aching Heart

It was past the hour of midnight;
she paused beneath the shady trees,
gazing in space at the moonlight,
feeling the kiss of a summer breeze.

Just a girl in the cool, sweet air,
cloaked in a mantle of thought.
A broken romance of yesteryear
and all the sorrow it brought.

Alone in the night, beneath a starry sky,
sadness will enter the heart.
Conscience will ask the reason why,
the reason two lovers should part.

Sometimes it's good to be quite alone,
to study the soul within.
Under the stars one can atone
and seek consolation in Him.

Thank You

Thank you for teaching me
the meaning of courage
as you have shown
that through your challenges,
every day, no matter
how they come your way.

Thank you for sharing your faith,
for it is in every moment that we live.
Thank you for your giving heart,
someone who has lost so much
but continues to give.

Thank you for teaching
me forgiveness,
as forgiveness
frees us to love.

This brings me to love,
as you have always shown.
Thank you for loving me
and being my big sister.

Wings of Fire

I watch you run like wings of fire,
as if you never tire.
I taught you well, as you taught me,
so God could set a path before me.
So our journey together has ended;
God has blessed another with your wings of fire.
So teach her well, my forever love,
as she takes you on her journey.
Run with endurance the race God has set
before you with Wings of Fire.

The Old Oak Tree

On the banks of a stream
where the meadows are green,
a stately old oak grows there.
A sight to behold,
majestic and bold,
kissed by the warm summer air.

Like a glorious shrine
it will stand throughout time,
there on the banks of the stream.
And one can feel blessed
when pausing to rest,
'neath the soft mantle of green.

For there in the shade
its branches have made,
the heart feels joyful and free.
Thoughts go back again
down memory lane,
while under the old oak tree.

To My Sister

In a bed of earth, you lie,
upon a grassy hill.
Sleeping in a dreamless sleep
that kissed your eyelids still.

There the feathered choristers
sing all through the day.
Bringing you sweet melodies,
in a soft and tuneful way.

When your bed is moistened
with sparkling morning dew,
that will be the tears, dear heart;
tears I shed for you.

Through the hours of sadness,
one thought I cherish best—
in the Master's loving care
we all find perfect rest.

So sleep, drear one, in silence,
beneath the soft green sod.

Tenderly we say goodbye
and give you back to God.

Book of Memories

Within my book of memories
are special thoughts of you,
and all the many nice things
you often say and do.

As I turn the pages
and recall each single thought,
I realize the happiness
that knowing you has brought!

There are memories of the times we've shared,
both bright and gloomy days.
There are memories of your kindness
and your friendly, thoughtful way.

There are memories of your laughter
and your cheery smile,
that add a bright note to each day
and make life more worthwhile.

There are memories of the things we planned,
each friendly little chat,

when we would get together
and just talk of this and that.

When I recall these memories,
as I go along life's way,
I find they grow more precious still
with every passing day!

My Last Days

As I lie on this concrete floor,
wondering why my master is walking out the door,
he hands my leash to a stranger
I do not know.

Barking, howling as to say,
why don't you want me anymore?
I was there for you, a companion and a friend,
the best you ever knew.
I even fetched you shoes.

I gave you loving kisses to show my affection
and lay by you when you had no one else.
I followed you wherever you went
because I was your protector
and just wanted to be near you.

I waited for you all day,
just wanting you to play,
but you didn't pay attention,
it seemed I was always in the way.

You were supposed to be my master,
the one I looked up to,
because I have no voice
I truly needed you.

Now my days are numbered
as I head for Rainbow Bridge.
I weep for you, my master,
as I wish you only knew that if I had a voice,
and you would have listened to your heart,
how much I could have given you.

Your loving companion…

Conscience

I was feeling quite alone,
one cool midsummer's morn,
and passed beside a thickly shaded wood.
So impressive and serene,
the beauty of the scene,
my inner thoughts there I stood.

Soon a gentle breeze
came floating through the trees;
the rustling leaves were music to my soul.
It seemed some magic hand
had made a fairyland;
entranced, I sat down on a grassy hill.

A few faint streaks of light,
adorned in silvery white,
lit up the fallen leaves upon the ground.
And overhead I heard
the song notes of a bird;
to me it was the sweetest kind of sound.

Oh, what a splendid place,

to meet God face to face,
and worship in that peaceful wooded shrine.
So I said a little prayer,
to the Master who was there;
forgive me for the sins I know are mine.

Mockingbird

I sat by your grave on the moistened grass
and asked God why you were taken so soon.
He did not answer.
My eyes filled with tears.

Then I heard a song.
It was a mockingbird that landed on your stone.
She sat a while and looked at me,
as if a sign from Heaven.

Then with wings spread she flew into the sky.
And then I knew it was an angel saying goodbye.

Reflections

Reflecting back to years gone by
and all the things I did and tried.

The simple times of baking with my mom,
or fishing with my dad in mountain streams,
where we spent our summers at Grandpa's cabin.

And how I loved the pony rides that turned
into lessons riding barrels at 6 years old.
The day I got my first horse—such happy times,
just he and I riding among the trees.

Then came loss and pain,
but God helped me through to live out my dreams.
And so I did rodeos, drill team, and parades;
I'm so thankful for all I did.

For these are reflections of God's plan for me.

Upon a Mountaintop

Sitting in my cabin
watching the fire burn,
flames of red and gold.
The fragrance of the pines;
I know this is my home.

The trails I hiked
and horse I rode.
I felt so near to God
in all His wondrous beauty.
The singing of the birds
flying high in the sky,
and in the hills
a buck, doe, and fawn
huddled, oh so near.

As these years come and go,
I will hold these memories
in my heart and soul.

Legacy of a Cowboy

He had a gift admired my many.
There wasn't a horse he couldn't ride,
and he trained many.

Not a steer he couldn't rope
or herding them from pasture.

I am thankful, for he taught me well.
For my dream was to win doing barrels at a rodeo,
and I did!

So ride 'em Cowboy in Heaven.
Through the fields you go,
with a smile on your face,
and with God's grace forevermore.

The Days Come and Go

The years they go so fast,
I pray to God your memory lasts.
My tears fall like rain,
and my body aches with pain.

I long for those days of talks and laughter,
and just hanging out being mom and daughter.
You called me your littlest angel,
that made me feel so special.

But I had no idea that God
would take you so soon.
I guess He needed another angel,
and He got the best, that I know for sure.

I keep in mind that you are not gone but just away,
till we meet again someday.
And there we will be,
with our heavenly Father through eternity.

A Grateful Heart

A grateful heart have I,
for today I didn't die.
You walked by where I lay in my lonely cage,
and reached out your hand.

You gave me a gentle stroke.
I looked at you with soulful eyes
and prayed you would say,
"I will take you home today."

Thank you for your loving heart,
to give me that forever home.
So now I look back, a grateful heart have I,
for today I didn't die.

[49]

Vacation Time

Vacation time will soon be here;
those are happy days.
When people leave all cares behind
and go their merry ways.

Some, no doubt, would love to camp
beside a mountain stream.
And cast for wily rainbow trout,
that is their fondest dream.

While others love the desert,
the cactus and the brush.
For lonely nights attract them
from city, noise, and rush.

The ocean, too, will have its call,
and crowds will travel there.
To bask upon the golden sands
and breathe salt laden air.

Give me the open country lane
and see the waving corn.
To listen to the meadowlark
in the early hours of morn.

And there amid the hedgerows

are wildflowers peeping through.
The petals shine like diamonds,
kissed by the morning dew.

Give me the open country;
it's paradise, I know.
And when vacation time arrives,
God willing, I will go.

A Beautiful Butterfly

Have you ever sat and watched
a butterfly in flight?
So delicate and beautiful,
yet so strong and determined.

God made everything
and look at this little miracle,
flying across fields of flowers
with such grace.

I know a beautiful butterfly
with beauty and grace,
who took a journey
longer than most.

Her name is Maddie,
now flying through
the fields in Heaven,
and resting in the arms of Jesus.

Courage

When you are faced with abuse and in harm's way,
have courage.
Do not fear for God is near.

If you think you have nowhere to hide,
and you want to leave, but you don't try,
have courage.
Let God take your hand and go.

Now don't look back with a hardened heart,
but look on to your dreams.
And God will give you courage.

Thoughts

Thoughts are like a tiny web
that creeps into the brain.
Some are good, some are bad,
and some bring grief and pain.

Jealousy, a nasty thought,
a good for nothing seed.
Avoid it as you would the plague,
or a worthless, filthy weed.

Envy, selfishness, and hate,
nothing could be worse.
They strangle all the good within
and become a deadly curse.

Anger, this you must control;
it causes much regret.
Words once spoken in this mood
are so hard to forget.

Thoughts of love and kindness;
thoughts that bring a smile.
Let them grow and blossom forth,
they make life worthwhile.

Happy thoughts are always good,

they ease someone in sorrow.
So plant a kindly seed today
and harvest reap tomorrow.

Keep in mind the Golden Rule;
this thought is so sublime.
To err is human, we all know,
but to forgive, Divine.

Welcome Home

A couple, aged and bent,
sit and contemplate the memories of their years,
dear to the heart they spent.

75 years and more,
the love between them,
oh so dear.

But when one goes home
to be with the Lord,
the other is left here to mourn.

Instead, rest assured,
she is at peace
in our Father's loving care.

Eventide

As eventide the setting sun
has sunk below the hill,
now the daily toil is done;
the old mill wheel is still.

Fleecy clouds pass overhead
beneath the azure sky,
tinted blue and gold and red
as they go floating by.

Phantom shadows softly creep
across the meadow green.
Little birds have gone to sleep;
all is peaceful and serene.

Fragrance from lilac trees
permeates the air,
as it mingles with the breeze,
spreading perfume everywhere.

To stand upon the soft, cool sod
and adore the countryside,
brings one near, so near to God,
in the calm of eventide.

A Gift from Above

My best friend is as black as coal
and eyes of golden.
He lives in my heart and soul
for 13 years and more.

I love it when he comes behind me
and paws my leg,
to let me know he is near
and will never leave my side.

And when I'm feeling down and out
he rests his head upon my lap,
to say it's okay,
everything will turn out right.

A best friend indeed,
I couldn't ask for more,
and thank you Lord
for allowing him to rescue me.

[59]

Acknowledgements

I would like to acknowledge God's goodness in my life. I am humbled by His generosity and love.

Much gratitude goes to Pastor Erik Sahakian for having faith in me to write this book.

As always, I owe a huge debt of gratitude to my husband who always encourages me to dream big dreams and achieve them. Love you forever.

I am thankful that my mother and both sisters encouraged me to write as a young girl. My mother and oldest sister are in Heaven now, and it is my hope that the writing of this book makes them proud.

About the Author

Bonnie Hopson was born in San Antonio, Texas. Being the daughter of an Air Force pilot (Lieutenant Colonel), she was fortunate to have lived in many different places.

At the age of six, she began taking riding lessons. Horses became her passion, as well as dogs. Then at thirteen, she was blessed with her own horse. From there she continued to train and compete in rodeos and gymkhanas. She enjoys the outdoors and being around animals has always been a blessing from God.

She lives in Southern California with her husband and two dogs.

Made in the USA
Columbia, SC
01 November 2021